THE REAL ESTATE JOURNEY
OVERCOMING OBSTACLES

A Guide to Overcoming Obstacles
of the Home Buying Process

THE REAL ESTATE JOURNEY
OVERCOMING OBSTACLES

A Guide to Overcoming Obstacles
of the Home Buying Process

ALICIA HURTT

Write Your Story Publishing, GLO LLC

Cherry Hill, NJ, USA

The Real Estate Journey: Overcoming Obstacles

GLO and WYS books may be ordered through booksellers
or bulk orders may be fulfilled by contacting the author or:
WYS Publishing, https://www.glotap.org
GLOInc2015@gmail.com
1-609-784-9698

All scripture references are taken from the Authorized King James
Version, unless otherwise noted.

All images are property of Bright MLS.

ISBN:
BUS054000   BIO026000   HOM025000

WYS Publishing pub date: February 2021

Printed in the United States of America

Write Your Story Publishing, GLO LLC
920 Haddonfield Road #716
Cherry Hill, NJ 08002

MY WHY

My God has blessed me beyond measure and continues to show me that He is the one and true living God. He has increased my wisdom, knowledge and understanding on a daily basis. He has given me the strength to be transparent and to develop a growth mindset personally, professionally and spiritually.

- My husband has always been a supporter of all my big dreams and visions. He has carried me spiritually when I fell short and has given me the courage to pursue my passion.

- My children, for giving me joy and fulfillment as a woman and mother and who have always given me the reasons to keep pushing and standing firm in my faith.

- My parents, for staying true to the word of God (Proverbs 22:6). Thank you for never giving up on me and continuing to provide nurturing even today.

- My ancestors, for paving the way for me and always being by my side as I walk this journey.

- My clients (YOU), for believing and trusting me with such a major decision, whether it is rentals, buying or selling your homes. You help me to reinforce that God is real, and if you ask sincerely he will grant your hearts desires!

TABLE OF CONTENTS

The Real Estate Journey

~ CHAPTER 1 ~

THE DESIRE

As a little girl, I always tended to have questions about everything that went on around me. I would ask questions about how my parents met; when they bought the house; where they lived before; how much the house cost; where they got the money, and if we were going to move one day. I remember asking so many questions while riding in the car, looking out of the window, and observing the cars and buildings we rode by.

My mom would answer, "Ask God."

I was puzzled by her response and frankly dissatisfied. I wanted to know everything at an early age! I was ready to solve problems and dissect every situation. This was a trait that has stuck with me along my journey.

> *"If any of you lack wisdom, let him ask of God, that giveth to all men liberally, and upbraideth not; and it shall be given him." ~ James 1:5*

I would listen attentively when watching TV shows and during "grown up" conversations to catch as much wisdom as I could. I felt like I had a right and needed to know what was going on at all times. I remember my dad having me open his bills and write out his checks monthly which taught me early on about finances. I looked forward to this task and wrote in my best penmanship for each and every check. Writing out the checks to pay bills made me feel a sense of leadership and responsibility. I had no idea the work that went behind my dad having the money to actually meet all debt obligations.

I remember going with my dad to buildings and sitting with my siblings as we waited for him to collect trash and clean up. I remember going to various homes with him and sitting while he made repairs. As a child, you were good as long as you had your snacks and entertainment.

My mom would rush off to work in the evenings and give us her expectations as she placed her lunch in her bag. My mom would return home after a 10 -12 hour shift and make the whole house wake up if the chores were not done as she expected. This was a hard lesson to learn for my siblings and me, as there were many nights of the same. My mom had to set the tone and ensure we had the foundation laid.

"Train up a child in the way he should go: and when he is old, he will not depart from it." ~ Proverbs 22:6

There was one time when we had to go out with my dad, and my hair was not done. My dad took that brush and put my hair in a bow. As I look back, that is a moment I cherish! Off we went to another job with my dad. These values stuck with me and planted a seed of work ethic that I had not known existed.

At school, I remember signing up to be a safety patrol officer. I loved it so much I became a captain! I remember having all the children in a straight line, waiting for the bus to come. I had two of the straightest lines and ensured everyone was quiet, not making too much noise. We had one child's grandmother with us every morning, and I remember her being so sweet and loving. She truly made our day. I recall praying at the bus stop at times as we waited.

"Don't follow the crowd, let the crowd follow you."
~ Margaret Thatcher

Every Tuesday and Sunday was dedicated to the Lord. We would be at Bible study, Sunday school and service promptly. I think that was the only time my mom would speed on the highway. We sat with Mother Henry and learned the books of the bible as well as many hymns that I can recall to this day. As a child, it was so hard to sit still for so long, but little did I know, the foundation was being laid. I never knew the true benefits of studying The Word, establishing a relationship with Christ and being covered under the blood until I started venturing out into the world having my own experiences.

I remember my first job at 16 years old was at Baskin Robbins in Landover, MD. My first day, I asked my trainer so many questions about the job, how he obtained the business, his life, how he started the work, what his goals were, and so much more!

I know for sure he needed a drink after my training was over. After the session, I needed to think through how I would be successful and how I would save the money I needed to buy my clothing and shoes. At that time, parasuco and princess jeans were the trend.

I cannot forget about my Air Force One and high top Reeboks as well. I needed to be able to keep gas in my car and to save for my own place. This was the start of understanding budgeting and how finances work.

During my middle school years, I remember the family packing up and moving to Capitol Heights, MD to share a duplex with my relatives. At the time, I did not understand that my parents were not just moving but becoming investors by renting our home. We stayed for about a year and then moved back to our home. The renters did not take good care of the home, and my parents had to go through the eviction process. It was costly to clean the home and make repairs to bring it back to the way it was prior to renting the home. This was a nugget that I would truly need later in life on my journey as a Real Estate Investor.

After graduating from DuVal High School in 2002, for a brief period, I attended Prince George's (PG) Community College with scholarship funds received by the Green Light Scholar program. I was very discouraged and anxious to do more, make more, and move out of my parents' home. I had a desire to have my "own." I saw the struggles of my parents and how hard they worked. I was determined to not only make my mark on the world but also to pay it forward so that my parents did not have to work that hard anymore.

I've worked at several companies in the banking industry, governmental agencies, a collegiate organization and public educational organizations.

I remember working as a teller and asking the people around me, one by one, how long they had been in their role; what the next steps were, and if they were satisfied where they were in life. You would think

I was doing a documentary because I was determined to find my purpose. While working in a small savings bank, I met a gentleman who explained to me that he could not give me the answers.

He went on to say, "You have to seek guidance from a higher power."

As a Christian, I thought I knew where he would land with his discussion, but it did not lead to an invitation to his church. Instead, he gave me a resource called *A Purpose Driven Life* written by Rick Warren. I read that book and was so inspired that I enrolled to obtain my degree.

I started with my Associate in Business Administration because I just knew that two years would be enough for me. During my coursework, I found a love for Business and started to dream like never before. The possibilities were endless as I developed business plans and learned about organizational structures. As I progressed through my education and career, I had a plan and became fueled to divert back to my foundation and refocus. I worked and went to school with the intention of progressing financially, spiritually, and personally.

It wasn't long before I met my spouse, and within two years, we were married. There was no option but to become homeowners as renting was not a long-term option for me. We rented for two years too long. I always had the desire to follow in the footsteps of my parents, so we saved and worked hard to build our credit. I utilized the family realtor, and he referred us to his lender. We started the home-buying process as many do— without much research, but driven to be approved and find our dream home. The process was truly emotional, and we were not prepared for all of the information, documentation and scrutiny facing us.

~ CHAPTER 2 ~

DREAM COME TRUE

WE ARE APPROVED!!!

It was now time to start looking for a home, based on our approval amount. We did not pay much attention to the required down payment or closing cost. As a young couple early in our careers, we did not have much assets or income, so we sought support from family. We started looking in PG County and learned really early that we could not afford to buy in that area.

Our realtor expanded the search to Baltimore, and we found our home in Dundalk, MD. It was an estate sale and, literally, only needed the carpet removed. We were not into the newly updated appliances and all the bells and whistles that attract certain buyers. The home had good bonds, was well maintained and had more than enough space for us to start our lives as a married couple. This was a dream come true!

Life was so good! We adjusted to the commute and learned the area quickly. We had our housewarming, family dinners and added personal touches to our home. We added our first pet to the family and watched as she ran around in the backyard. There wasn't much more to add to make us more satisfied.

Then the unthinkable happened, and our dream became a nightmare! I lost my job, and soon after, my spouse did as well. At 21 and 24 years old, we had no idea what was in store for us financially. We fell behind on the mortgage, and the letters started to come from the bank. We were ashamed, disappointed in ourselves and had too much pride to reach out for assistance.

We did not know our rights as homeowners. As with many new homeowners, the excitement of the settlement process and receiving the keys deter you from asking pertinent questions of your lender. We had the big packet and did not think to look through the documents or to reach out to our lender for options. We allowed our youthfulness, pride, and inexperience get in the way of finding a way to save our right to remain in our home.

"Wisdom is the principal thing; therefore get wisdom: and with all thy getting get understanding."
~ *Proverbs 4:7*

We struggled for months, working temporary positions and searching for work. This situation not only broke us individually, it put a strain on our relationship due to the built up stress and uncertainty of the coming days. As new homeowners, we did not understand our rights. We did not know that there was a process the bank had to undergo before we could be forced out of the home.

~ CHAPTER 3 ~

IN JUST A YEAR

In just a year of purchasing our home, we were packing up a truck and moving into a rental home in Middle River, MD. There were so many unanswered questions, and no one in our circle had the answers. At least, that's what we thought. We were too embarrassed, frustrated and deflated to really know. We felt like we let down, not only ourselves, but everyone around us. We did not think to seek help and did not know our rights as homeowners. As soon as the letters started coming in, we started to react instead of doing the research. We had blindfolds on and started working on plan B. We were in reactive, survival mode. We did not want to go home or ask anyone for assistance. With our limited thinking and experience, we thought we had to figure the situation out.

We were the first to become homeowners among our circle. Therefore, we had not heard of anyone going through this situation, and we were not going to be the first to communicate it. The calls did not stop coming from the bank, so we knew for sure we needed to do something to make the situation go away. I filed bankruptcy, and we moved into a rental townhome and started to rebuild. We paid rent on time and established positive credit on our own. Due to having credit challenges, these accounts carried high interest rates. Our spending habits remained the same, and we did not see the pattern recurring that led to foreclosure and bankruptcy.

While renting, we had the opportunity to reestablish as a married couple and restart our career paths. We did not have to worry about maintaining the property, paying taxes, or paying for a home warranty. Renting took away much of the stress that came with homeownership. As long as we promptly paid our rent, we were able to reside at the residence.

> *"Life is really simple, but we insist on making it complicated." ~ Confucius*

We rented three different places over several years and drew exhausted from not having the benefits of homeownership. That peace of coming home to your own home was missing and desired. We started doing research to find a way to purchase another property. We applied to lenders and were told, "No," time and time again. We were doing the same things over and over with no avail.

> *"The definition of insanity is **doing the same thing** over and over again, but **expecting different results**."*
> ~ *Albert Einstein*

After filing bankruptcy, we worked hard to rebuild my credit worthiness. It took much discipline and sacrifice. I used my spiral notebook to track my progress and restructure my plans monthly. There were many apps and guides to assist, but going back to the basics truly worked.

~ CHAPTER 4 ~

THE REBUILD

As a renter, we had the flexibility of just paying rent, renter insurance and utilities with no other obligations. For many, this would be a comfortable time period. For me, there was always a still, small voice driving my ambition to do better, grow, work harder and build. No matter the road block or situation, I have always stayed the course and pushed forward. There were definitely moments of doubt; however, I never remain in that place long. I have strong belief and maintained my daily prayer, which gave me strength. My belief in God and relationship with the Lord has kept me grounded.

"No weapon that is formed against thee shall prosper; and every tongue that shall rise against thee in judgment thou shalt condemn. This is the heritage of the servants of the Lord, and their righteousness is of me, saith the Lord." ~ Isaiah 54:17

I remember my mom telling me the story of her rebuild and how she went back to the basics to ensure the household bills and their personal bills were strategically paid down to obtain a loan to purchase their first home in Landover, MD. I used the same method by pulling out a sheet of paper and writing down all of our household obligations and our individual obligations. We strategized and started executing our plan to rebuild.

Bill	Due Date	Balance	Minimum Payment	Comments (ie. How much paid - plan to payoff)
My Credit Card	10/1	$350	$30	Paid 9/30 $50- payoff by Dec.
My Line of Credit	10/15	$1,500	$100	Call to change payment date
Spouse Credit Card	10/5	$550	$35	Ask for settlement or reduction of fees

I did research on how people repaired their credit and started to implement some of the techniques. We worked hard to pay down our bills and ensure bills were paid on time. I wrote letters to the credit bureaus, disputing accounts. I contacted creditors to establish payment arrangements and settled out accounts. It definitely took time, discipline and patience. It was a tedious task, but it worked well with improving my credit score and being able to manage bills.

~ CHAPTER 5 ~

A SECOND CHANCE

Rentals can be found all over the internet using branded companies and newspapers. My husband stumbled across an ad from a private owner who was renting a home off of Pulaski Highway in Baltimore. The price was reasonable, and we were  seeking to move from renting an apartment. The owner offered the option to buy the property, and that was very appealing as we were still rebuilding. We signed a standard rental and an option contract with the purchase price and deposit amount. This was known as a rent to own (RTO) agreement or rent with the option to purchase. We were able to rent the home and had the first right to purchase at a set price.

We lived in the home and had a few issues that were quickly resolved by the landlord. The neighborhood was not as desirable, and community concerns started to surface. One day, I received a call at work saying the neighbors' home was on fire, and I rushed home to make sure everything was alright. I called the landlord and asked if she had any other properties that she would be willing to allow us to rent with the option to purchase. She was very understanding but did not have any other properties. She explained later that she was compelled to assist my family, and she sent me a list of properties she would be willing to purchase on my behalf.

This was not a typical response, and I was ecstatic! I started looking and found the neighborhoods and homes to be undesirable. She called me to say there was a home she had just found that was not on the market that I may like. I went to see the home and fell in love. It was a detached, raised rambler with the original wood floors in great condition. The neighborhood was quiet, and I could envision living comfortably there.

My landlord purchased the home and found someone else to rent the previous home. We lived in the new purchase for a few years and finally received good news that we could qualify to purchase. The transaction was not as stressful as the first home, but there were moments of uncertainty as we went through underwriting. Needless to say, we owned the home and started on our path of a second chance.

Our relationship as a married couple grew, and so did my desire to become a mother. We had been married for more than five years and had not been successful. I was always super transparent, and as I shared my story, a co-worker opened up and gave  me a referral to see a specialist. At the time, I had really good benefits and found out that almost all of the expenses were covered. We went through three rounds of in vitro fertilization (IVF) and were unsuccessful. The news took a toll on me as a woman and my relationship with God. I could not understand why I could not become a mother. I had so much love to give, and I thought I was on the right path. I went to church regularly, studied The Word, and was faithful to my servant hood and calling.

As I pushed to try a fourth time, my husband finally said, "Enough is enough." He told me we were not going through the process again. He saw how much I went through and did not want me to push anymore. He said to me, "If God wants us to have a child, He will do it himself."

I looked into adoption and other options but had to come to the same conclusion. I had to muster up the faith and know that it was not my will but God's.

> *And He went a little beyond them, and fell on His face and prayed, saying, "My Father, if it is possible, let this cup pass from Me; yet not as I will, but as You will." ~ Matthew 26:39*

I had moments that were very dark for me. As a woman, having a child was a part of my role that I could not fulfill. I felt like a failure and truly did not know where to turn. I had moments of anger towards God. I was depressed and lacked faith. This was truly a time when I needed prayers from others to cover me.

> *Confess your faults one to another, and pray one for another, that ye may be healed. The effectual fervent prayer of a righteous man availeth much.*
> *~ James 5:16*

~ CHAPTER 6 ~

STEPPING OUT ON FAITH

There are outcomes that can be predicted and those that truly test your faith. My husband took the lead and listened to a message God gave him. He sat me down and told me that we were going to have a child and needed to move closer to family for support. I was truly not in a place to receive or hear anything as I went through my dark moments of losing two embryos. I followed my husband's lead, and we put the home on the market for sale.

We reached out to our last realtor who helped us with the rent to own purchase of the home. Looking at the market and how quickly we wanted to sell the home, the two did not match. The listing price did create traffic by buyers, but no offers were presented for over a month. During my search online, I found a company that bought homes for cash and settled quickly.

The home buying specialist visited our home and made an offer. We would have the opportunity to sell the home without owing anything additional and move back home to PG County. This was very exciting news for us. The sell was not going to be a traditional buy and sell transaction; it was called a "subject to." The home buying specialist would resume paying my current loan, and the deed would transfer to the new owner. This was uncharted territory for us, but we felt a sense of comfort and trust for the home buying specialist. He was true to his word, and we successfully went to settlement.

We moved back to PG County and found out a few months afterwards that we were pregnant with our first daughter! This was confirmation that God truly spoke to my husband. In that moment, I could do nothing but praise and glorify the Lord. This was a blessing! Our prayers were answered!

> *"Has the Lord as great a delight in burnt offerings and sacrifices. As in obedience to the voice of the Lord? Behold, to obey is better than sacrifice, And to heed [is better] than the fat of rams. ~ 1 Samuel 15:22-24*

We still had not started our search to purchase a new home, and with a baby on the way, we needed a solid plan in place. We rented a few homes and were able to start parenthood; however, we still desired to have our own home.

~ CHAPTER 7 ~

CREATIVE APPROACH - RTO

We were back on the hunt to obtain homeownership once again. I reached out to the home buying specialist because he was also a realtor. We went through financing and found a home. Unfortunately, due to my student loans, the financing fell through. This was truly disappointing to say the lease. We did not give up at all. My husband and I made a decision to keep building and restoring so that when the time came we would be ready to purchase.

Having gone through this before, we decided to rent a home and pay down on the loan until we could qualify again. We found another local realtor, and she was really nice. We looked at several homes, and then she recommended a rent to own program so that we had more options.

She explained that the program allowed us to rent for up to five years as we work to purchase the home. The requirements were lower than obtaining a mortgage, and we had the benefit of selecting a home on the market for sale. This was very good news!

We completed the application and received approval within a couple of days. It felt nice to look for your home and not be limited to rental properties. There are good rentals but even better homes for sale. We found a real nice one-level home with most of our desired features: the yard was a nice space; it had a garage, and there was a shed for my husband's storage. Additionally, this neighborhood was pleasantly quiet.

We selected the home, paid the two months deposit, and our realtor did the rest. We received a call a few days later to inform us that we got the home! We prepared for move in and could not thank God enough for the blessing of being one step closer to owning a home again!

We loved the home and even shared great memories with the family, hosting dinners and gatherings. As our love grew, so did our family. We were running out of space and needed a bigger home. We reached out to the program and realtor to see if we could find a bigger home. Of course, because we still had blindfolds on during the process, we did not know that one can only participate once in the program as the goal is to purchase the home selected.

We had not yet completed any of the work to support purchasing a home and needed to make a decision as I would deliver our next child really soon. We contacted the same realtor, and she was able to find us another rental. This time around, we could not stay on this path, and it had to be the very last rental for the family. Besides, soon after we moved in, I had the baby and was expecting another shortly afterwards.

We hunkered down and started the process over again. This time, it was different. I started searching for fixer uppers, for sale by owner, owner financing and other creative ways to obtain a home. I ended up reaching out to a former co-worker who had recently become a realtor. She referred me to her colleague that specializes in Investment properties and fixer uppers. We met and strategized on how the dream of homeownership could be reality once again.

~ CHAPTER 8 ~

THE NEXT CHAPTER

L ittle did I know that history would be in the making for our family. I started studying for my real estate license while on maternity leave and focused more on the plan set forth by my realtor. We met a credit specialist and a lender whom I could truly connect with as a mother and woman in real estate. They both gave us a plan to meet our timeline of three to six months, as our third child would be due soon. As time went on, our realtor followed up and held me accountable as he received updates. I felt like we had a team supporting us to achieve the goal. That kept me motivated and calm during the process.

Going through the process, we saw many homes but none of them really had the feeling of home. We settled for a home in Waldorf, MD but were denied due to multiple offers. Clearly, that was not our home. We were disappointed but kept pushing. By this time, I was getting further along in my pregnancy. I remember sitting in a home, that was well staged but weirdly designed and saying that we have to find our home. We sat in the home, and my realtor started looking up homes. We called our lender to crunch numbers and headed to see one last house. We drove so much that my realtor soon needed gas!

As we pulled up to the next home, my husband had a little twinkle in his eye. There were big front and back yards that reminded him of his hometown country living. I walked through the home and stared out the front window, praying and talking to God. I wanted him to guide me, as I knew my emotions and time constraints would play a role in the decision. My husband and I looked at each other, and we knew this was the house. We told the realtor we would call with a decision by the next day and ended up telling him via text that night.

As we anxiously waited, we received the call that we probably need to rethink our offer as the owners had multiple offers. We went to our maximum approval amount and submitted the offer. Shortly afterwards, we received word that our offer was accepted! We jumped for joy!

The underwriting process was a true roller coaster ride. We got all the way to closing day and had to request an extension due to more verification needed on an account that caused my score to dip. The team strategized; I had to contact creditors for verification and write letters of explanation. I received a call informing us that despite all our efforts, we could not obtain the loan. We were knocked down yet again! We decided to start looking again in a lower price range the very next day. I received an email from a creditor and forwarded it to the lender. Literally thirty minutes or so later, my lender issues an approval! I called my realtor, and he jumped on the phone with the realtor for the home we were previously denied for, and they allowed us to continue the process and rescind the release of contract.

We are so greatly appreciative of the realtors, lenders, and credit specialists that worked to support our family in purchasing our homes. They saw our blindfolds and walked us through every step of the way. This was my first lesson learned as a real estate agent: to ensure that I am supporting my client every step of the way.

~ CHAPTER 9 ~

PAYING IT FORWARD

As my knowledge of real estate grew, so did my desire to help more people like myself. I knew I had to focus on paying it forward as my realtors, credit specialists and lenders did for me. As first time homebuyers, sellers and renters, you wear blindfolds and need the guidance. Knowing this, I started researching ways to reach clients who need the guidance. I did extensive searches online, attended trainings and watched many videos from seasoned real estate agents.

I have helped families with credit scores below the criteria desired; however, using creative strategies, they were approved to rent homes and reestablish credit. I have helped families who previously were denied to overcome hurdles, and now they own homes. I've helped families, who needed to quickly sell their homes, receive asking and above asking price. I go hard for my clients and never give up because no one gave up on me!

I created groups on Facebook, Twitter and Instagram called "Rent to Own Maryland - Alicia Hurtt" and have been able to assist many families over the past three years. The group is still growing and so is the need to help others on the path to homeownership. I will continue to tell my story and encourage others to push past hurdles that come up in life. My family was able to overcome, not once or twice, but many times, and I am confident that you can and will.

It may take a year or a few years but, stay the course and do not give up on yourself. Be specific in your desires and speak them into existence. No matter the hurdle there is always a way to overcome. At times you may feel defeated but, you can see from my journey that God never failed. I could never imagine that going through so many trials would land me and my family in our current situation. You will look back one day and say the same thing. Take a few nuggets from this book and start applying them to your current situation. Remember, there is more than one way to slice that apple.

> *"Obstacles don't have to stop you. If you run into a wall, don't turn around and give up. Figure out how to climb it, go through it, or work around it."*
> *~ Michael Jordan*

NUGGETS

1. ***Do Your Research***

    a. *Understand the programs you can qualify for based on your profession, income and desired neighborhood(s).*

    b. *Understand the rate and how it changes over the course of the loan.*

    c. *Understand the lenders process for late payments and modification of the loan.*

    d. *Understand your rights as a homebuyer.*

2. ***What are in the Loan Details***

    a. *Understand how your rate is calculated.*

    b. *Understand if you are being charged points for the loan.*

    c. *Understand how your credit score impacts your rate.*

    d. *Understand the type of loan you are receiving (ie. fixed, balloon, adjustable)*

    e. *Understand the period of time you have to lock into the loan.*

3. **Rights as a Mortgagee**

   a. Understand who you should contact with questions after you close.

   b. Understand the fees associated with servicing the loan (if any).

   c. Understand the forbearance and modification process.

   d. Understand how you can pay down the loan sooner.

   e. Understand the amortization.

4. **Renting - When is it good?**

   a. Are you in the military and subject to relocation.

   b. Unsure about where you want to live?

   c. Building your credit.

   d. Working on stable employment.

   e. In a stage in life that you do not want to maintain a home.

   f. Waiting for two years after bankruptcy.

5. **Private Owners vs. Organizations**

   a. Flexibility in the terms.

   b. What is in the fine print.

   c. Is the deposit refundable.

    d. *How long are you given to purchase?*

    e. *Is the contract legal?*

    f. *Seek guidance from a Real Estate professional.*

6. **Write Your Vision and Make It Plan**

    a. *Be specific (i.e. how long, how much money to save, steps in process).*

    b. *Be attainable*

    c. *Be realistic*

    d. *Have faith*

7. **Be Open to Other Options**

    a. *Research other ways to purchase.*

    b. *Be open minded.*

    c. *Seek guidance from a Real Estate professional or Attorney.*

    d. *Remember to read the fine print.*

8. **Subject to - My Way Out**

    a. *Understand the loan remains in your name but, the deed transfers*

b. *Understand you go through the closing process and depending on the structure of the deal you may receive cash at settlement.*

c. *A fast way to transfer ownership and obligation to the loan.*

d. *Make sure you receive everything in writing.*

9. **Credit Matters Even After Home Purchase**

a. *Establish your routine and stick to it.*

b. *RULE: If you cannot pay off the card next month do not buy the item.*

c. *Live within your means.*

d. *Use credit only for emergencies.*

e. *Have a plan and stick to it no matter what.*

10. **RTO - Rent to Own**

a. *There are many programs to assist.*

b. *Research and understand how long you have to purchase the home.*

c. *Deposits go towards the purchase of the home and may not be fully refundable.*

d. *Read the contract and understand it.*

e. *Seek guidance from a Real Estate professional or Attorney before signing.*

f. *Some programs provided incentives for timely monthly payments.*

g. *A creative way to obtain homeownership.*

11. **Do Your Work**

   a. *Ensure your credit is ready or seek out a credit specialist.*

   b. *Shop for the best lender and ask questions.*

   c. *Understand what you desire in a home.*

   d. *Interview Real Estate professionals for the best fit.*

   e. *Stay committed to the process.*

12. **Credit Repair**

   a. *Research the steps in maintaining a good score.*

   b. *Stay the course and be disciplined.*

   c. *Seek out a professional to support you if you cannot do it on your own.*

13. **Savings**

   a. *Always keep at least 3-6 months in the bank at all times.*

   b. *Try to keep it separate and act as if it is not in your account.*

c. *Build every pay period even if it is less than you desire.*

d. *Seek out programs to support offsetting your down payment or closing costs.*

14. **Patience and Prayer**

   a. *This is a journey and it does not happen for everyone overnight.*

   b. *Remember "no" does not mean that it will not happen it just means not right now.*

   c. *Stay the course and seek guidance when you are uncertain.*

   d. *Use daily affirmations to build motivation and strength during the process.*

15. **Always Share Your Testimony and Help Others**

   a. *You never know who needs to hear your story.*

   b. *You may save someone and not even know it by sharing your testimony.*

   c. *It takes guts but your blessing will come through helping someone overcome their hurdle by hearing your story.*